They Are Los

Written by Joseph Perlas

Illustrated by Andy Wilson

13

Consonant *Jj* /j/	Consonant *Xx* /ks/
Jan	box
Jen	Fox
just	Max

High-Frequency Words

are	look	they
he	said	was
here	she	where

1

Dad said Jan was in the box.

Where is Jan Fox?
She is lost!

Dad said Max was in the pen.

Where is Max Fox?
He is lost!

Dad said Jen was in the bed.

Where is Jen Fox?
She is lost!

They are not lost.
Just look here!